Jewish
Synagogue

Angela Gluck Wood

W
FRANKLIN WATTS
LONDON•SYDNEY

This is the symbol sometimes used
to represent the Jewish faith.

For Adam Lowenthal

This edition first published 2005

Franklin Watts
96 Leonard Street
London EC2A 4XD

Franklin Watts Australia
45-51 Huntley Street
Alexandria NSW 2015

© Franklin Watts 1998

Editor: Samantha Armstrong
Series Designer: Kirstie Billingham
Illustrator: Gemini Patel
Religious Education Consultant: Margaret Barratt, Religious Education Teacher Advisor
Religious Consultant: Laurie Rosenberg, Board of Deputies of British Jews
Reading Consultant: Prue Goodwin, Language and Iinformation Centre, Reading

Dewey Decimal Classification Number 296

A CIP catalogue record for this book is available from
the British Library

ISBN 0 7496 6206 9

Printed in China

Contents

Synagogues around the world

◁ This synagogue is in Germany.

A **synagogue** is a place where Jews meet to worship God and to study. Some synagogues are small and simple. Others are large with a lot of decoration. There are synagogues all around the world.

Jews believe in one God. The special day each week for Jews is called **Shabbat.** It lasts from Friday evening until Saturday night. Lots of Jews go to the synagogue on Shabbat.

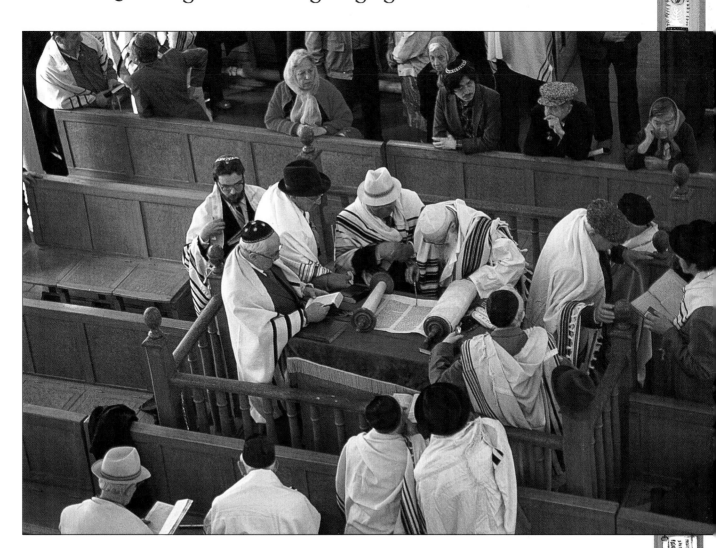

Inside a synagogue

Every synagogue has a large cupboard called an **Ark.** Inside the Ark are the **Torah scrolls.** Scrolls are books written on **parchment** and rolled up. The **Torah** is the special book for Jews.

◁ When people face the Ark, they are facing in the direction of Jerusalem. Jerusalem is an important city for Jewish people.

There is also a platform, called a **bimah.**
The person leading the worship stands on
the bimah. In most synagogues men lead the
worship but, in some synagogues women
may also lead prayers.

◁A teenage boy and girl
are on the bimah together,
reading the Torah.

IN·MEMORY·OF·DAVID·QUIXANO·HENRIQUES·1804-1870·

The Ark

The Ark is a special cupboard where the Torah scrolls are kept. Each scroll has the Torah written on it. The Torah is a collection of Jewish laws, stories and teachings about God.

On Shabbat and other ▷ festivals one of the Torah scrolls is taken out of the Ark and read. The Torah is used to help guide Jewish people in their daily lives.

10

The Eternal Light

Above the Ark is the **Eternal Light** or **Ner Tamid.**
It can be an oil lamp or an electric light.
It is kept alight. It reminds Jews that the
Torah is always there and that God lives forever.

The curtains on ▷
the Ark are closed.
The Ner Tamid
shines above the Ark.

A Torah scroll

A Torah scroll is written by hand. It is in **Hebrew**, the Jewish language that has been used since ancient times. A **yad** is used to point to the words. Scrolls are attached to wooden rollers. Some are rolled up and put inside a cloth cover.

◁ The scrolls have a silver breast plate, called a hoshen, over the cloth cover.

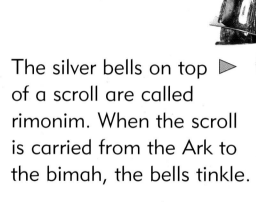

The silver bells on top ▷ of a scroll are called rimonim. When the scroll is carried from the Ark to the bimah, the bells tinkle.

12

A Torah scroll is undressed before it is read. First the silver bells are taken off. Then the pointer is removed, then the breast plate and finally, the cloth cover.

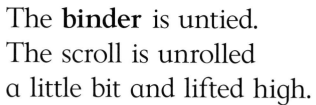

The **binder** is untied.
The scroll is unrolled
a little bit and lifted high.

The person holding
it turns four ways
so that everyone
can see the Torah.

15

Reading from the Torah

Before and after the Torah is read, one person sings a **blessing** to thank God for the Torah. The people in the synagogue join in for part of the blessing. While the Torah is being read, everyone follows carefully to make sure that the words are read exactly as they are written down.

◀ When people read from the scroll, they follow the words with the yad. 'Yad' means 'hand' in Hebrew.

Getting ready for prayer

For morning prayers, all men and older boys wear a shawl called a **tallit**. In some synagogues women and older girls wear one when they pray too. A tallit usually has blue or black stripes and fringes on the edges.

There are long, thin fringes called **tzitzit**, on each corner that are knotted in a special way. Tzitzit remind Jews about God and the Torah.

◁ The tallit is often kept in a cloth bag. The Hebrew on this bag spells 'tallit'.

18

◁ Jews put on their tallit before morning prayers begin. Some Jews cover their head and face with the tallit for a moment and pray or think in private.

When they bring the tallit ▷ down on to their shoulders, they are ready for morning prayers.

Praying

There are three **services** a day in the synagogue. Jews can pray on their own but they usually pray together.
Most of the prayers say 'we', 'us' and 'our'.

Any adult Jew can lead the prayers.
Sometimes a **rabbi** leads them.
A rabbi is a teacher and preacher.

Jews mostly pray in Hebrew. In some synagogues some prayers are in the ordinary language of the country.

Ten Commandments

The **Ten Commandments** are the most important part of the Torah. Most of them are rules. When they are read from a scroll, everybody stands up.

This is a simple version of the Ten Commandments:

1. *I am God. I love you and I give you freedom and hope.*

2. *Only pray to God.*

3. *Use God's name only at special times.*

4. *Every week, celebrate a day of rest, peace and happiness.*

5. *Care about your parents.*

6. *Love life and living things.*

7. *Protect your family.*

8. *Do not steal.*

9. *Be honest.*

10. *Do not get jealous.*

The first words ▷ of the Ten Commandments are written in Hebrew on the wall of this synagogue. They are in the shape of two stone slabs because that is how they were first written down.

22

Jewish art

There are no statues and no pictures of God in the synagogue. Jews believe that God does not have a body and that it is wrong to worship people. Most Jewish art is about the Torah, the land of Israel and the first Jewish temple from long ago.

◀ This candlestick has seven branches, like a tree. It is called a menorah. There was a menorah in the ancient temple in Jerusalem.

24

This girl has painted the ▷ Old City of Jerusalem on a piece of cloth which she is making into a tallit.

▲ The vine in this picture stands for the land of Israel and the Jewish people because the branches of a vine weave around each other.

◁ This is called a Magen David which means Shield, or Star of David. There were 12 tribes in Israel and the star has 12 edges.

25

Synagogue activities

Most synagogues have classes for children, after school or on Sunday mornings. They learn about the Torah, Jewish history and festivals and how to read Hebrew. There are classes for adults and families too.

◁ These children are making pictures to celebrate the Jewish festival of Hanukah. Here they are making pictures using sand.

On a day before ▷ Hanukah, these children learn how to make olive oil and light the Hanukah lights.

Glossary

Ark	the special cupboard where the Torah scrolls are kept
bimah	the platform where the person leading the prayers stands and where the Torah scrolls are read
binder	a sash that is tied around a Torah scroll to stop it unwinding
blessing	words of thanks and praise
Eternal Light	a light above the Ark that shines all the time
hoshen	a silver breast plate that goes on a scroll
Hebrew	the language of the Jewish people
Ner Tamid	the Hebrew word for the light that shines above the Ark
parchment	a kind of paper made from animal skin that is thick but not stiff
rabbi	a Jewish teacher and preacher
rimonim	the bells on the rollers of a Torah scroll

scroll	a book that is made of a length of parchment and rolled up
services	meetings of Jews in the synagogue
Shabbat	the special time for Jews, lasting from Friday evening until Saturday night
synagogue	a community centre where Jews meet to pray and study
tallit	a shawl worn for saying prayers
Ten Commandments	an important part of the Torah, telling Jews about God and how to live their daily lives
Torah	a collection of Jewish laws, stories and teachings about God
tzitzit	the corner fringes on a tallit that are knotted in a special way
yad	the pointer that looks like a hand and is used to follow the words in the Torah

Index

Photographic acknowledgements:
Cover: Steve Shott Photography; Ann and Bury Peerless.
Insides: P6 Fabrizio Bensch/Impact. P7 Bruno Barbey/Magnum.

P24 Ann and Bury Peerless.
P25 Top: Carlos Reyes-Manzo, Andes Press Agency.
P25 Bottom left: The Hutchison Library.

All other photographs by Steve Shott Photography.
With thanks to The West London Synagogue and United Synagogue, Hendon.